Germy Science

The Sick Truth about Getting Sick (and Staying Healthy)

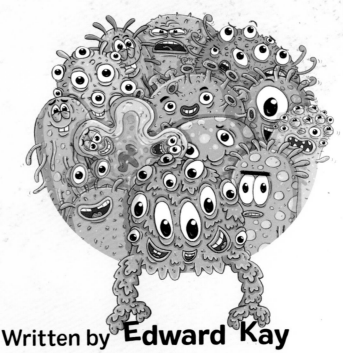

Written by **Edward Kay**

Illustrated by **Mike Shiell**

KIDS CAN PRESS

Wash Your Hands!

You can't tell by looking, but the book you're holding is covered in germs! But don't be alarmed! Compared to your skin, these pages are an oasis of sterility. Unless it's a copy that you're reading in a doctor's waiting room. In which case, *ewwww*, gross, it's DEFINITELY covered in germs. And now your fingers are, too! No need to panic. Just don't touch your face until you've washed your hands. By the time you finish reading this book, you'll know why! Because you're about to go on an amazing journey into the world of germs, life forms so tiny that even though they've changed the course of human history, we didn't even know they existed until just a few hundred years ago. So get ready to become a master of microbes!

Contents

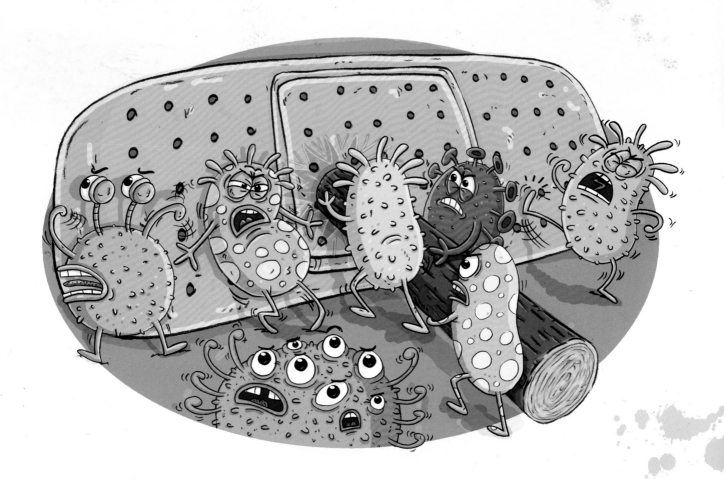

Germs Are Everywhere!

You can't avoid germs. They're everywhere — in the air, the soil, the water, your classroom, your bedroom and even on this book! They are all over you, too — on your skin, in your mouth, ears and nose, inside your guts and, yes, in your bum. Nobody knows for sure how many germs live in us and on us, but the best guess is that it's somewhere between 100 trillion and 200 trillion per person. That's more than the number of drops of water in 100 000 Olympic swimming pools!

But germs are so tiny that they are invisible to us unless we're looking through a microscope.

See this red dot?

It can hold about the same number of germs as the biggest stadium in the world can hold people!

Even though they're too small to be seen, germs make their presence known. If your nose has ever been filled with snot because you had a cold, or you wish it were filled with snot so you couldn't smell someone's bad breath, you've had a close encounter with germs.

Hello, Germs!

Germs get a bad rap because some of them can make us sick or even kill us. But they aren't all bad. If you've ever enjoyed some cheese or yogurt and then digested it along with all your other food, you've experienced germs firsthand. Germs do many things, both helpful and harmful, depending on the type of germ and where it is. Some can turn milk sour and make our stomachs ache or cause ear infections, pimples, chicken pox and cavities. But other germs help us absorb vitamins, make soil fertile for growing food and fight off other **microbes** that would make us ill. Without germs, you might never get sick, but you also wouldn't live to enjoy your good health for very long, because you literally can't survive without them. So say hello to these tiny but influential inhabitants of our bodies and our world.

Great-Grand Germs

Germs are an ancient life-form — older than Neanderthals, mastodons, sharks and even dinosaurs! They've been found in ancient Egyptian mummies and in *T. rex* fossils. Germs appeared on Earth billions of years ago. And we're lucky they did! They transformed the planet.

Germs first lived in the oceans. About 2.7 billion years ago, **Cyanobacteria**, also known as blue-green algae, began using sunshine, water and carbon dioxide to produce chemical energy. It's a process known as **photosynthesis**, and it produces oxygen. Before that, there was little oxygen on Earth. So if you've taken a breath of fresh air recently, you can thank microbes for it. Just try not to think of it as inhaling germ farts.

Humans are even distantly related to germs. Scientists who have analyzed the **DNA** of an **organism** named **Archaea** believe that we, and all other animals, may have evolved from it. Perhaps that's why bacteria enjoy camping out on us so much — they're like relatives who come to visit and then never leave.

Location, Location, Location

Certain germs, such as *Escherichia coli*, better known as *E. coli*, are good in some places but bad in others. *E. coli* lives in our intestines, where it helps us digest our meals. Without it and other germs, we wouldn't get the nutrients out of the food we eat, and we'd die of starvation. But if *E. coli* gets out of our guts and finds its way into other parts of our bodies, it can make us very sick. That's why it's important to wash your hands carefully with soap and water after you've gone to the bathroom. You want to make sure that any dangerous *E. coli* on your fingers gets flushed down the drain.

What Exactly *Is* a Germ, Anyway?

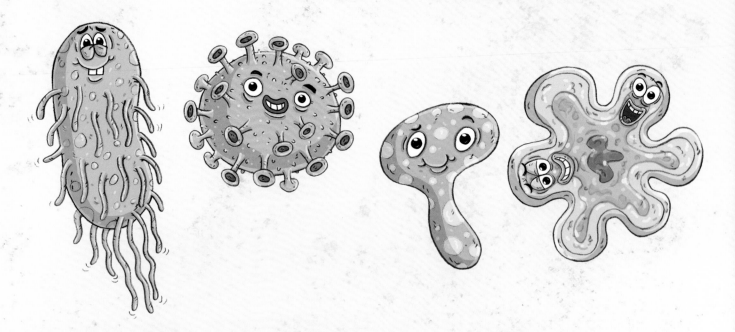

Germ or *microbe* are general terms we use for four basic types of organisms: bacteria, fungi, protozoa and viruses.

Bacteria come in all different shapes and can live almost anywhere, even in radioactive waste! Most bacteria are harmless, but others are responsible for some of the nastiest diseases humans can catch, such as tetanus, cholera and leprosy.

Fungi can be found in a comforting bowl of mushroom soup, on a tasty pizza or, if you're unlucky, growing on you in the form of an infection called athlete's foot. Fungi are parasites that absorb the nutrients they need from living or dead plants and animals. Some fungi cause fatal diseases, such as meningitis. But we use others to create important medicines, including penicillin, a drug that has saved millions of lives.

Protozoa live in water or in the body of another organism. All higher life forms, including you, have at least one kind of protozoa living in them. Most are harmless, but some cause diseases, such as sleeping sickness and malaria. Others are extremely helpful. Tiny protozoa called zooplankton are the blue whale's main source of food. Other protozoa are used in sewage treatment plants to clean our water.

Viruses are tiny but tough. Some can even survive in outer space! A virus needs a host such as a plant, animal, bacteria — or a person. The virus injects its DNA into the host cell, then takes it over and makes copies of itself, destroying the cell and making the host sick. But not all viruses are bad. Like some fungi, certain viruses can be used as medicines to treat cancer and to kill harmful bacteria, for example.

Scientists believe that there are at least 9000 different types of germs in the average home. There may be between 10 million and 1 billion species of bacteria in the world. An estimated 320 000 types of viruses infect mammals. And there are at least 120 000 kinds of fungi and 50 000 species of protozoa.

There are about three pounds of germs in your body at any one time. That's the same weight as your brain!

How Germs Were Discovered

Germs discovered us long before we discovered them. Some of them were busy making us sick. Others were hanging out on us and in us because our bodies supply all the yummy things they like to eat, such as sweat, poop and dead skin. But for most of human history, because we couldn't see germs, we weren't even aware that they existed.

So how did people explain sickness? Most people realized that some sick people could pass their illnesses to others, but they weren't sure how. Many others believed that illnesses were caused by things like evil spirits, planets aligning in particular ways or something called **miasma** — vapors in the air that somehow made people sick. The ancient Greeks didn't fall for that though. They believed that people became ill because the god Zeus was angry at humans for stealing fire!

Microbes and Monsters!

Rabies is a viral disease that affects mammals, including humans. Symptoms include aggression, hallucinations, sensitivity to light … and a terrible urge to bite. Sound familiar? The terrifying sight of people infected with rabies may have given rise to the first vampire stories. Meanwhile, African trypanosomiasis, or "sleeping sickness," might be what inspired legends of zombies. The disease is spread by a protozoan called *Trypanosoma brucei*. When people are bitten by a tsetse fly infected with this protozoan, it enters their bodies and eventually finds its way to their brains. It makes victims act like mythological zombies: sleeping during the day, walking and talking with difficulty and behaving aggressively.

Bad to the Bone?

After hearing about zombies, vampires and deadly diseases, you could be forgiven for thinking that all germs are bad to the bone. But you'd be wrong. And not just because germs don't have any bones!

The fact is that there are lots of germs that help us. For starters, germs are the sanitation workers and recyclers of our world. Without germs, dead animals and plants would pile up all around us until we were buried in them. Yuck! Germs break down that organic matter so new plants can use it as energy to help them grow. Those plants in turn provide food for us and other animals. Good germs even keep us healthy by killing bad germs!

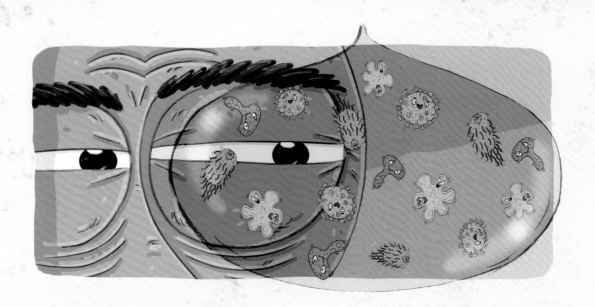

It's Alive!

The first clue that it wasn't gods, planets, vapors or vampires causing all that trouble came in 1673. That's when an amateur Dutch scientist named Antonie van Leeuwenhoek gazed into a water droplet. Using a microscope he'd built himself, he saw tiny creatures in the droplet and named them **animalcules**. He estimated that it would take 10 000 of them to make up the volume of a single grain of sand. Van Leeuwenhoek had discovered germs.

Fascinated by these tiny creatures, he looked for them in other substances, including saliva. Van Leeuwenhoek reported that he saw "with great wonder that in the said matter there were many little living animalcules, very prettily a-moving. The biggest sort had a very strong and swift motion, and shot through the spittle like a pike [a type of fish] does through the water. The second sort spun round like a top." He also scraped dental plaque off the teeth of an old man who claimed to have never once cleaned them and saw "an unbelievably great company of living animalcules, a-swimming more nimbly than any I had seen." Not only had van Leeuwenhoek discovered germs, he'd also found an excellent reason to brush and floss your teeth! But he didn't make a connection between these tiny life forms and infectious diseases.

Moldy Medicine

Van Leeuwenhoek wasn't the first scientist to make a discovery that he didn't fully understand. Doctors in ancient Greece and India treated infected wounds with mold, and in 1640, a British scientist named John Parkington recommended using mold to treat infections. If you scraped your arm or knee in seventeenth-century Poland, your doctor might have gone a step further and treated your wound with a mixture of wet bread and spiderwebs, both of which can contain mold spores.

But it wasn't until 1928 that Scottish scientist Sir Alexander Fleming proved that a type of mold called penicillin could kill harmful bacteria. It does so by preventing them from reproducing. When bacteria exposed to penicillin try to make copies of themselves to infect our bodies, they instead burst apart and die.

Ignaz Semmelweis, Super Sleuth

In 1846, a Hungarian doctor named Ignaz Semmelweis faced a grim mystery in his hospital's maternity ward. Many mothers there died of an infection known as puerperal fever or childbed fever. Babies at the hospital were delivered by both doctors and midwives, women specially trained for the job. Semmelweis noticed that when midwives delivered the babies, mothers usually survived. But when doctors delivered babies, their mothers often died from fever.

Semmelweis discovered that some doctors were performing autopsies on dead bodies and not washing their hands before delivering babies. Their patients were the ones who died. *Was something harmful being transferred from the dead bodies to the healthy mothers?* wondered Semmelweis. He pestered the doctors to clean their hands with a chlorine and water mixture. The death rate from childbed fever dropped drastically, from nearly one out of every five patients to one out of every fifty.

Unfortunately, some doctors were offended by Semmelweis's suggestion that their poor hygiene was to blame for the death of their patients, and he lost his job. Today, we know that the culprit was a bacterium called *Streptococcus pyogenes*, which the doctors unknowingly transferred from the corpses to the mothers who were unlucky enough to be in their care.

Sour Grapes and Tiny Shapes

Semmelweis was right, although it would be a few years until someone demonstrated the connection between germs and illness. And it wasn't because of sick people but sick wine! In 1856, French winemakers hired scientist Louis Pasteur to find out what made certain wines spoil and taste bad. Examining spoiled and unspoiled wine under a microscope, Pasteur saw tiny objects — bacteria — in the spoiled wine but not in the unspoiled wine. His detective work proved that bacteria were the problem.

Pasteur reasoned that if bacteria could make wine sick, it could also make people sick. To prove his theory, he heated two flasks of germ-filled broth until the liquid was so hot that it killed the germs. He sealed one flask and exposed the other to the air. Soon, the exposed broth was once again crawling with germs, while the sealed container stayed germ free. This proved that airborne germs could multiply rapidly in food or living organisms. It led Pasteur to develop a process in which foods such as milk are heated up to a temperature that kills bacteria. We call it **pasteurization**.

Spontaneous Maggots

Amazingly, many scientists resisted Pasteur's ideas. Instead, they believed in something called the spontaneous generation theory — the idea that life, including germs, emerges suddenly and spontaneously from nonliving matter. For example, some scientists thought that mice were created by rotting grain and that maggots were somehow made by spoiled meat.

Not only do germs not emerge from nonliving matter, they also prefer to make their home on living things. A patch of your skin the size of a coin has 30 million germs on it — more germs than there are people in all of Australia!

Three Infected Mice

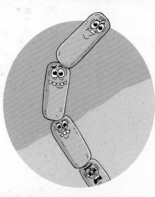

In the late 1800s, a German researcher named Robert Koch finally persuaded the scientific community that germs caused disease. He did so by taking the blood of sheep infected with anthrax and injecting it into healthy mice. Soon, those mice also became sick with anthrax. Koch examined their blood under a microscope and found that it contained rod-shaped bacteria that hadn't been there before. Those bacteria were also in the blood of the infected sheep.

Koch discovered that the anthrax bacteria created a spore: a cell that quietly waits, doing nothing, until the right conditions appear. The anthrax spores were tough and resistant to heat and cold, so they could survive in soil for years. Then, if an animal came along and ate plants grown in the contaminated soil, the spores would come to life in the animal's blood and begin to reproduce, causing the disease to once again spread.

Even then, many scientists refused to believe that germs infected humans. They thought only animals were affected. But in 1882, Koch discovered the bacteria responsible for tuberculosis, a disease that has killed millions of people throughout history. Medical science at last accepted the germ theory of disease.

Viruses, which are generally among the tiniest germs, weren't discovered until the 1890s. That's just a few years before Orville and Wilbur Wright succeeded in becoming the first humans in history to take to the skies in an airplane — no doubt with billions of germs tagging along.

How Germs Make Us Sick — and How Our Bodies Protect Us

Although germs are happy to hitch rides on airplanes, they're also very good at getting around without them. Some germs float in the air. Others are sprayed at us by sneezes and coughs. Many live in water and get into our bodies through our ears, nose and mouth. Soil is teeming with germs that can infect us if we fall and cut ourselves. Some germs just sit around on things like doorknobs, waiting to be picked up. They can also get into us from contaminated food or from other animals, such as fungus in pigeon droppings. Some of the deadliest diseases, such as malaria and bubonic plague, are transmitted through bites from infected insects. If it seems like germs are everywhere … well, it's because they are!

That's Sick!

Infections happen when viruses, bacteria, fungi or protozoa get inside our bodies and multiply. Every type of germ does something different. Viruses kill or damage our cells by hijacking them to reproduce themselves.

Bacteria can multiply so quickly — from a few to a few million in less than a day — that they crowd out our own cells and stop them from working properly. Some bacteria make toxins that poison us or break down and consume our cells. For example, necrotizing fasciitis, better known as flesh-eating disease, is a particularly nasty bacterial infection that treats our bodies like a giant buffet, dissolving us so the invaders can more easily chow down and multiply.

Harmful fungi are rare, but they can damage our lungs or cause deadly inflammation in other parts of our bodies. They also produce **enzymes** that digest our cells.

Protozoans make us sick by robbing us of our nutrients and damaging our cells. For example, malaria is caused by a type of protozoa, which typically enters your body through a mosquito bite. It travels to your liver and lays its eggs in your red blood cells, which eventually burst, releasing more protozoa, which then invade more of your red blood cells.

> About 30 percent of your poop is bacteria! So remember to wash your hands after using the bathroom.

Fighting the Good Fight

Fortunately, our bodies have many ways to fight germs, starting with something called the innate immune system, meaning the one you are born with, as opposed to the defenses you develop as you grow up. The first line of defense in your innate immune system is a little something called skin. It's like a suit of armor that keeps tiny invaders from getting at your insides. However, a cut or a burn creates an opening where germs can get in. That's why it's so important to clean and disinfect a wound immediately and cover it with a bandage.

Our bodies have other ways to protect us. The hairs in your nose trap germs. When you exhale, your breath blows them away. Ooey-gooey earwax is another weapon in your body's germ-fighting arsenal. It snares any crafty little germs that try to sneak in through your ear canals.

People used to think that if you didn't cover your nose and mouth when you sneezed, your soul might get sneezed out along with the snot. That's why to this day, when someone sneezes, people often say, "bless you" or "gesundheit," which is German for "good health."

A Cup of Snot a Day Keeps the Doctor Away

Snot is one of our greatest weapons in the fight against germs. Your body produces about a cup of it every day! You probably didn't realize that because you swallow most of it. Yes, it's true. (Sorry!) Snot contains **proteins** that kill germs and enzymes that chop up bacteria. It also traps germs and carries them down to your stomach, where your digestive juices destroy them.

You've probably noticed that when you have a cold, your nose produces even more snot than usual. That's to trap the viruses. A thin layer of mucus in your throat does the same thing. And when you sneeze, air, germs and other little bits of stuff in your nose are fired out at about 150 km/h (93 m.p.h) — the same speed as a hurricane!

Plan B

Even when germs manage to get inside us, we usually don't get sick. That's because our bodies have a powerful second line of defense called an adaptive immune system. It's the part of our immune system that develops special abilities when it is exposed to germs. Think of it as your own private army, ready to fight off all invaders.

When your cells detect germs, they send out a chemical distress message. White blood cells swallow up and destroy the incoming germs. Your blood also produces special proteins called **antibodies** that can tell the difference between your body's cells and the intruder. They attach themselves to the invading germs, signaling more white blood cells to attack. You'll get sick with a cold or a flu for a while, but your body eventually wins the battle and you're healthy again.

Your adaptive immune system will always remember that particular germ. If it ever comes back, you either won't get sick or you'll have milder symptoms and recover more quickly.

Germs are different in different parts of the world. That's why sometimes you get an upset stomach or diarrhea when you travel. You've just met some of the microscopic locals, and your immune system hasn't prepared a defense against them yet.

Mutants from Inner Space

You may be wondering, "If my immune system recognizes intruders, why do I catch a cold or flu again?" Germs mutate and evolve, just like other life forms. So a germ might not look exactly the same the next time your body has to deal with it. It takes a while for your immune system to recognize the mutated intruder and learn how to fight it. In the meantime, you get sick.

Some of the symptoms that we associate with illness, such as fevers and rashes, are actually your immune system trying to fight off the invaders. For example, fevers are your body's way of trying to kill germs using heat.

Sometimes Caring Means *Not* Sharing

It's not nice to share germs, so here's some health etiquette. Cold viruses can remain infectious on your skin for at least an hour and on surfaces like doorknobs for 24 hours. If you cough or sneeze, cover your mouth and nose with a tissue or the crook of your elbow so you don't get it on your hands or cuffs and spread it further. Wash your hands regularly. Twenty seconds with soap and water will do the trick. And when you're sick, stay home so you don't make other people sick, too!

Keep It Clean!

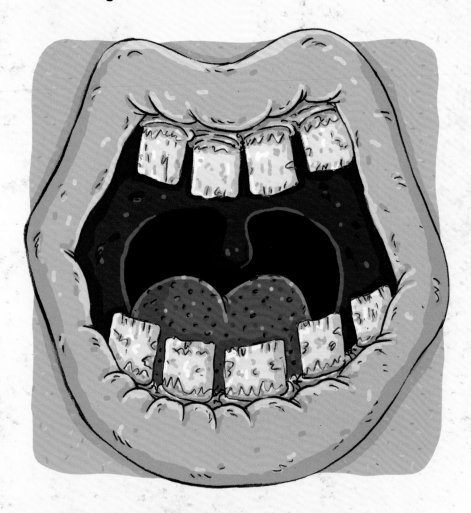

Washing your hands and face keeps germs from building up on your skin and getting inside you. Brushing your teeth and flossing is important, too, because around a thousand types of bacteria live in your mouth. Remember van Leeuwenhoek and the old dude who never cleaned his teeth? Bacteria love to munch on the sugars in the tiny fragments of food left behind in your mouth.

The clear or yellowy-white gunk that builds up on your teeth is called plaque. It's a layer of bacteria. Plaque reproduces until you've got millions of bacteria merrily munching in your mouth, then pooping acid onto your teeth. That acid attacks tooth enamel and causes cavities. If you don't brush and floss, plaque poop will eventually rot your teeth.

People actually used to die from tooth infections caused by bacteria. A 5000-year-old corpse dug up in Switzerland showed signs of gum disease so bad that the microbes had found their way into his hip bones.

Stay Safe!

There are many ways to protect yourself from germs. Keep raw meat refrigerated and put cooked food or leftovers in the refrigerator as soon as possible. In a warm environment, a bacteria population can double in size every 20 minutes!

Picking your nose is a bad idea if you don't want germs to get inside you! First, your fingernails can cause tiny scratches in your nostrils that let germs in. Second, those germs will now be on your fingers and you can spread them to other people by touching things — *like this book*. Ewww!

Ditto for picking pimples. They're caused by bacteria blocking the pores in your skin. So leave them alone! Your body can deal with bacteria better by isolating it inside a pimple. If you pick zits, you're just letting all those bacteria escape and get all over your skin.

The irrational fear of germs is called **mysophobia**. When a nasty illness is going around, it's good to physically distance, wear a mask and wash your hands regularly. But people who suffer from mysophobia are so scared of germs all the time that they may disinfect cutlery, refuse to have physical contact with other people and wash their hands over and over again. Some therapists cure their patients of mysophobia by taking them on the subway and making them lick the handrails!

An Ounce of Prevention

Many infections can be prevented through **immunization**, also known as **inoculation**. This process exposes your body to a dead or weakened version of a germ so that your immune system can build a defense against it. The first immunization may have been performed more than 2000 years ago in China, years before germs were discovered, to fight smallpox.

Smallpox is a viral disease that was once common and widely feared throughout Asia and Europe. It sometimes killed more than half the people it infected. People who survived often went blind or were badly scarred. Seeking a prevention, some unknown person long ago was inspired to grind smallpox scabs into powder, then blow it up the noses of people who hadn't yet caught the disease. Those dead smallpox cells stimulated their immune systems to create a defense. Later, if they encountered active smallpox viruses, their bodies would be able to fight them off. This process is known as **variolation**, after the variola virus that causes smallpox.

In the 1600s, Chinese emperor K'ang-hsi decreed that inoculations against smallpox were mandatory, despite the protests of people who were squeamish about having powdered scabs blown up their noses. Later, K'ang-hsi proudly wrote that he had saved millions of lives.

Pustule Power

Europeans and North Americans learned another method of variolation from people in Turkey. In the early 1700s, Lady Mary Wortley Montagu, the wife of the British ambassador to the Ottoman Empire, learned that many Turkish people took powdered smallpox scabs or fluid from smallpox pustules and rubbed it into scratches on the skin of people who had never been infected. By being exposed to weakened smallpox cells, their bodies could prepare a defense against stronger smallpox infections.

When Lady Montagu returned to England, she had her children immunized before physicians of the royal court, who didn't believe it could work. But it did. More tests were conducted on condemned prisoners, who were promised freedom if they survived. Just like Lady Montagu's children, they lived, and variolation became common throughout Western Europe. However, it wasn't completely reliable. Sometimes people treated this way became ill and died, and sometimes they spread the disease to other people.

In West Africa, people practiced a similar method of immunization. When some Africans were enslaved and brought to North America, the practice spread throughout that continent. During the American Revolution, George Washington ordered that his soldiers be variolated to protect them against smallpox.

Don't Have a Cow

In the late 1700s, English doctor Edward Jenner pioneered a more reliable form of immunization known as **vaccination**. Jenner was inspired after hearing a milkmaid boast, "I shall never have smallpox, for I have had cowpox." Cowpox is a viral disease that affects cows and can be transmitted to humans. But it's much less serious than smallpox. Jenner took pus from the lesions of another cowpox-infected milkmaid and scraped it into a cut on the arm of an eight-year-old boy. He waited six weeks, then exposed him to smallpox. The boy was unaffected.

In Europe at the time, smallpox killed 400 000 people every year. So governments there and in North America immediately promoted Jenner's work. Within four years of his experiment, 100 000 Europeans had been vaccinated. The practice eventually became common worldwide.

> The last known naturally occurring case of smallpox was in Somalia in 1977.

Herding Germs

Jenner's success inspired other researchers. The next breakthrough came in 1885, when Louis Pasteur — the bacteria-wine guy — developed a rabies vaccine. Over the next century, scientists created **vaccines** to prevent other illnesses, including tetanus, cholera, polio and measles.

How important is immunization? In 1900, one out of every six children born in the United States died before their first birthday, largely because of germ-related diseases. Of the five who survived, one more would die before their fifth birthday.

Had you been born then, you'd have had a one-in-three chance of dying before you were old enough to read this book.

Now, vaccinations are so effective that some deadly diseases are virtually nonexistent because of **herd immunity**. That's when so many people have been vaccinated — say 19 out of every 20 — that viruses have trouble finding a host. The people who are vaccinated protect those who aren't. However, children are still especially vulnerable to infection, so make sure you get vaccinated and keep your vaccinations up to date!

Before vaccines were invented, some people took their children to "pox parties." These parties exposed them to infections such as chicken pox and measles, which are more serious when you get them as an adult. For the record, birthday parties are probably a *lot* more fun than pox parties.

Germ Warriors

Throughout history, humans have demonstrated an unfortunate knack for creating all sorts of weapons to help us smite one another.

The relationship between war and germs began accidentally. When ancient armies went on the march, germs went along with them. As often happens when large groups of people gather together in unsanitary conditions, diseases broke out. Often, more soldiers were killed by illnesses than combat. It was only a matter of time until it occurred to military leaders to use that deadly potential against their enemies. Today, we call this **germ warfare** or biological warfare.

Rotten to the Corps

In 400 BCE, Greek soldiers reportedly dipped arrows in rotting bodies to create toxic projectiles. The ancient Roman and Persian armies dumped dead animals into their enemies' water supply. But the most spectacular use of early germ warfare had to be at the 1346 Siege of Kaffa, a port city on the Black Sea. A Mongol army was trying to persuade the Italian defenders of the walled city to surrender. The Italians had other ideas, and the siege dragged on for three years, with neither side giving in.

The combination of overcrowding and unsanitary conditions inevitably led to illness. The Mongol commander, Jani Beg, was understandably perplexed to see thousands of his soldiers dying horribly painful deaths without getting a chance to disembowel or decapitate their opponents. But he must have heard that old saying, "If life hands you lemons, make germ-filled lemonade for your enemies."

Jani Beg ordered his army to stop catapulting boulders and instead launch a different projectile over the walls: the dead and decomposing bodies of his infected soldiers. This made life quite unpleasant for the Italians, who were kept busy dumping rotting Mongols into the Black Sea. Still, the Italians refused to surrender, and Jani Beg eventually gave up. However, Italian sailors who returned home unwittingly brought a little souvenir with them: the bacteria responsible for the Black Death. It unleashed the worst plague in history — but more on that later.

Banning the Bugs

In 1925, the League of Nations (the forerunner of the United Nations) banned the use of biological weapons. But it didn't ban nations from making them or stockpiling them, so many countries did.

Baa-Baa-Baa-Boom!

During World War II, the British experimented with making bombs containing anthrax, which not only kills animals but can harm people, too. It didn't go too well. In 1942, the bomb was tested on sheep on Gruinard Island in Scotland. When the sheep became infected and died, someone had the not-terribly-bright idea of blowing up a nearby hill to bury them. Unfortunately, one of the dead sheep was blown into the ocean and washed up on shore elsewhere, where it infected other sheep.

After World War II, the Soviet Union (now Russia) and the United States both developed lethal germ weapons but never used them. In 1972, more than 100 nations signed the Biological Weapons Convention to ban making germ-based weapons. But there may still be rogue nations developing such weapons, as well as terrorist organizations eager to get their hands on them. Germs are an unpredictable ally that can kill friend and foe alike, which is perhaps why — fortunately — they haven't been very popular as military weapons.

Only one nation used germ warfare in combat during World War II. The Japanese army spread plague and typhoid throughout several Chinese cities, killing thousands of people.

The Deadliest Enemy

Of course, even without germ weapons, wars kill plenty of people. Nearly 20 million soldiers and civilians died in World War I, which lasted from 1914 to 1918. But ironically, an even bigger killer emerged in the last few months of the conflict: the 1918 flu. It was spread around the world by millions of soldiers. The flu eventually infected one out of every three people on Earth. An estimated 50 million people died of the disease. Germs proved to be even deadlier than military weapons.

Germs That Changed History

You probably know all about COVID-19, a disease caused by a type of virus called a coronavirus. If you've ever had a cold or the flu, you've already experienced one version of a coronavirus. As you've read elsewhere in this book, germs are always mutating, or changing, so that our immune systems don't recognize them right away in order to fight them off. COVID-19 was caused by a type of coronavirus that mutated into a new form. Because it was so new, at the time when this book was written, scientists hadn't yet developed medicines to treat it or vaccines to prevent it. So it spread quickly to people all over the world. When a lot of people in one area or community get sick, it's called a *plague* or an *epidemic*. When the disease spreads to other countries and continents, it's called a *pandemic*. And as you're about to read, this was not the first time in history that germs mutated and caused a pandemic, and it won't be the last time. But by being careful and taking proper hygiene precautions, the odds are strongly in your favor that you'll get through it just fine. Wash your hands thoroughly, stay six feet away from other people in public areas and wear a mask in a crowd, and you'll keep other people safe, too.

When in Rome

Ever heard the expression "Win the battle but lose the war"? That's kind of what happened to the ancient Romans. In the second century, Roman armies conquered Mesopotamia, a region in the Middle East. They gained new territory and wealth, but they also got something they hadn't bargained for: a highly contagious deadly disease!

When they returned to Rome, soldiers who had been exposed to the virus spread it to people in the city and eventually to much of the Roman Empire. Between 165 CE and 180 CE, five million people were killed by what was dubbed the Antonine Plague. The Roman army was literally decimated: one out of every ten soldiers died in the pandemic. The loss of life was so severe that some historians consider this plague to be the first event that seriously weakened the Roman Empire, bringing about its eventual collapse.

Second-Place Plague

The second-worst pandemic in history, the Plague of Justinian, occurred in 541 CE and hit the Byzantine Empire especially hard. It was spread throughout the Mediterranean by ships carrying rats that had fleas. The fleas were in turn infected with the plague bacteria. A particularly unpleasant effect of this plague was that people's fingers turned black and died as the bacteria dissolved their cells. By the time it was over, the plague had killed an estimated 25 to 50 million people. And that's only the second-worst plague in history!

The Deadliest Plague

Remember the Siege of Kaffa? It probably touched off the Black Plague — also known as the Black Death — the worst pandemic in history. Between 1347 and 1351, it killed as many as three out of every four residents of Europe and Asia. People thought the world was ending.

The Black Plague was caused by *Yersinia pestis*, bacteria carried by infected fleas. *Yersinia pestis* blocks a flea's gut. This makes the flea so hungry that it bites any available host, including humans. In a desperate attempt to make space for food, the flea barfs up the contents of its stomach, spreading even more germs.

To make matters worse, medieval sanitation was sketchy. In London, for example, the streets were bare earth, topped with generous helpings of human and animal excrement, animal entrails and rotting food. This created the perfect breeding ground for rats and the plague-ridden fleas that snacked on them.

The Black Plague's symptoms included swollen lymph nodes, fevers, chills, nausea, diarrhea and extreme weakness. Victims often bled uncontrollably from their mouth, nose, rectum and skin. Black scabs formed on the sores, which is how the pandemic got its name.

Desperate Measures

People invented many strange theories to explain the Black Plague. Some thought it was caused by unusual planetary movements. Others blamed their innocent Jewish neighbors, many of whom were forced to sign false confessions before being executed. There were the usual "punishment from God" believers, too.

Doctors tried all sorts of cures, such as cutting their patients' skin to bleed them and giving medicines containing "powdered unicorn horn," arsenic and mercury. If you didn't like the idea of swallowing deadly poison, your doctor might instead place the shaved butt of a live chicken on your inflamed lymph nodes to draw out the infection. You might not be surprised to learn that none of these antidotes worked.

Shaking the Foundations

The Black Plague killed so many people that it changed the power structure of European society. Under the **feudal system**, a small number of landowners ruled the peasants who farmed the land. When the plague finally ended, there was more work than workers. Wealthy landowners couldn't find enough people to tend their farms. Many peasants moved to towns and cities, where employers paid higher wages.

Atlantic Crossing

Germs arguably were more effective than military might to help Europeans colonize the Americas. When Columbus arrived in 1492, millions of Indigenous people were living there already and had been for thousands of years. They weren't keen on the idea of foreign invaders waltzing in and taking over. But they'd never been exposed to many of the diseases that the Europeans carried, so they had no immunity to the new germs. The result was catastrophic.

An Unseen Enemy

In 1520, the Aztecs soundly defeated a small army of Spanish soldiers at Tenochtitlan, now known as Mexico City. But among the Spanish dead was a smallpox-infected soldier. The Aztecs who handled the soldier's corpse became infected, too, and the disease quickly spread.

Historians estimate that in Tenochtitlan alone, three to four million Aztecs died from diseases introduced by the Spaniards. In other Aztec cities, as many as 95 percent of the people were killed by the new germs — an even higher percentage of people than were killed by the Black Plague. Germs did what the Spanish army had been unable to do: destroy a powerful empire.

Deadly Deception

In the 1700s, the British military decided to use germ warfare to defeat the confederation of Indigenous nations taking part in Pontiac's War. The British gave their enemies blankets that had been intentionally infected with smallpox. It is unknown whether the plan was successful. So many millions of Indigenous people died from smallpox as a result of other contact with Europeans that it is impossible to say which source of the virus killed them.

We do know that these diseases were devastating. Historians think that by 1600, barely a century after Europeans arrived, the Indigenous population of North America had fallen by 90 percent. Incredibly, it even affected the climate. Indigenous people farmed huge portions of the continent. When they died and their farms were left untended, forests reclaimed that land. The new growth drew so much carbon dioxide out of the atmosphere that scientists think it may have set off something called the Little Ice Age, causing rivers in Europe to freeze over and, ironically, leading to crop failures and famine there.

The Future of Germs

For most of human history, we didn't even know that germs existed. So it's not surprising that we're still finding out lots of things about them. And just like other types of organisms, from penguins to people, germs mutate and evolve. That's why you never develop complete immunity to colds and the flu. Most germ mutations just lead to inconveniences like getting the sniffles once in a while or needing a flu shot each year. But sometimes, germs evolve in truly scary ways.

Mutant Superbugs

Germs are constantly evolving. Recently some bacteria have adapted to absorb NDM-1, a resistance gene that makes them immune to antibiotics. That means that doctors don't yet have effective drugs to treat infections caused by those new bacteria. The NDM-1 gene is particularly worrisome because it can spread from one species of bacteria to another through contact, like when they're sloshing around together in a puddle of dirty water. The good news is that researchers are working on ways to treat illnesses caused by so-called superbugs.

Too Much of a Good Thing

Antibiotics, a type of medicine, have saved millions of lives. They've also been used in livestock feed for about 50 years to prevent cows, chickens and other farm animals from getting sick. Unfortunately, all that exposure to antibiotics has allowed some bacteria to evolve resistance to them. So some drugs are losing their effectiveness in fighting bacterial infections. But germs themselves may ultimately come to the rescue. Researchers are experimenting with using viruses to attack and kill superbugs.

The Battle Continues

New and deadly germs, such as the Ebola virus, are emerging all the time. Struggles between humans and germs might always exist, but thanks to science, humans usually win, at least eventually.

Consider HIV/AIDS, an epidemic that emerged about 40 years ago. It has killed 36 million people, making it the fourth-worst epidemic in recorded history. The virus weakens the human immune system over time so that other germs and diseases have a chance to take hold. Although there is still no cure, drugs called antiretrovirals prevent the virus from reproducing and damaging a person's immune system, allowing people with HIV/AIDS to live long, healthy lives.

Go with Your Gut

In the fight against bad germs, there's lots of good news, too. It's too early to be certain, but some researchers believe that microbes in our **gastrointestinal tract** might affect our appetites and eating habits, causing us to crave certain foods. Some of our gut microbes might make us want to eat fatty things. But others might encourage us to eat healthy foods. Certain gut microbes may even affect our moods and cause depression. Scientists are experimenting with replacing those bad microbes with the good microbes that make us feel better and want to eat healthy things.

And that's not the only way germs can help us be healthy. In the future, viruses may be scientifically modified to recognize and kill cancer cells, as a form of cancer treatment.

Tiny Crime Fighters

Someday, germs may even help put criminals behind bars. Researchers say that soil has a germ **fingerprint** so specific that just a tiny smudge on a person's shoe can potentially place them at a crime scene. Since we all have unique groups of microbes living on us, a criminal might accidentally leave their own "germ fingerprint" on a weapon or other item that ties them to a crime scene. Investigators may even be able to establish a murder victim's time of death based on what microbes are living in the victim.

Germs That Clean

Researchers are also exploring industrial uses for germs, such as using bacteria to make fuel cells, drugs and new kinds of plastics. Someday, germs might also be used to clean up the environment. Researchers have already discovered bacteria that eat plastics and oil. Others might be used to neutralize dangerous pesticides and herbicides.

A Germy Goodbye

One thing is certain: for as long as we've been on this planet, humans have had a close relationship with germs, and we will continue to do so. There are thousands and thousands of species of germs out there that may hold the key to curing diseases and keeping our planet healthy. Germs may be tiny, but they're nothing to sneeze at!

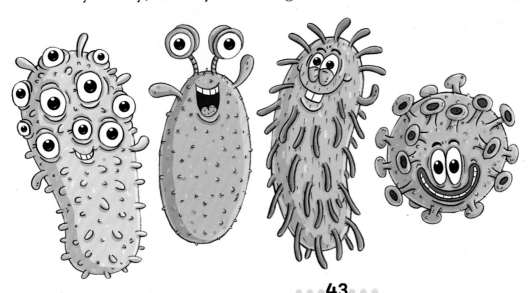

Glossary

animalcule: a term used in the 1600s to describe a tiny organism that can only be seen with a microscope

antibiotics: a type of medicine, such as penicillin, that treats infections by killing bacteria

antibodies: proteins formed when the body detects an invader, such as a harmful germ. Antibodies attach themselves to germs and destroy them.

archaea: single-celled organisms similar to bacteria

bacteria: tiny, single-celled organisms that live in water, soil and human or animal bodies and can only be seen with a microscope

COVID-19: a respiratory illness caused by a coronavirus that causes fever, cough, shortness of breath and other symptoms. First identified in China in 2019, COVID-19 spread around the world in 2020 and became a global pandemic.

cyanobacteria: microscopic organisms found in both freshwater and saltwater that convert sunlight into food and produce oxygen through the process of photosynthesis. Also known as blue-green algae.

DNA (deoxyribonucleic acid): material in a living thing's body that holds information about how that living thing looks and behaves

enzymes: molecules in the cells of living things that speed up chemical reactions

epidemic: an outbreak of disease that affects many people in a particular community

feudal system: a system of social and political organization in medieval Europe in which land was controlled by wealthy families, and peasants farmed that land in exchange for protection and a place to live

fingerprint: something, such as a unique characteristic or trait, that sets apart a person or thing

fungi: organisms that absorb the nutrients they need to survive from living or dead plants and animals

gastrointestinal tract: the part of the human digestive system made up of the stomach and intestines

germ warfare: the act of using germs as weapons, either to kill enemies or destroy their crops and livestock. Also called biological warfare.

herd immunity: when a large percentage of a community is immunized against disease, protecting the few people who aren't immunized

immunization: the act of making a living organism resistant to a disease

inoculation: the process of introducing a weak or dead version of a virus, such as smallpox, into the body in order to stimulate the immune system to create antibodies that protect against that disease

miasma: vapors, or bad smells, in the air that were thought to cause diseases

microbes: very small organisms, such as bacteria, fungi, protozoa or viruses, only visible through a microscope

mysophobia: the irrational fear or hatred of germs and dirt

organism: a living being

pandemic: an outbreak of disease that affects many people across multiple communities or regions

pasteurization: a method of sterilizing liquids by heating them up to kill bacteria, invented by French scientist Louis Pasteur

photosynthesis: a process in which plants combine sunlight, water and carbon dioxide from the air to create the glucose (sugar) they need to grow and give off oxygen

plague: any disease that spreads across a wide area and results in many deaths

protein: a chemical compound that helps maintain the bodies of plants and animals

protozoa: small, single-celled organisms that have a nucleus and can only be seen with a microscope

vaccination: a process in which a vaccine is introduced into your body to encourage your immune system to learn how to protect your body against a specific virus

vaccine: a dead or weakened version of a virus

variolation: the process of inoculating someone against smallpox by deliberately infecting them with the virus

virus: a very tiny organism that invades the cells of living things in order to multiply itself

Index

Further Reading

Alexander, Lori and Vivien Mildenberger. *All in a Drop: How Antony van Leeuwenhoek Discovered an Invisible World.* New York: HMH Books for Young Readers, 2019.

Cline-Ransome, Lesa and James Ransome. *Germs: Fact and Fiction, Friends and Foes.* New York: Henry Holt and Company, 2017.

Eamer, Claire and Marie-Ève Tremblay. *Inside Your Insides: A Guide to the Microbes That Call You Home.* Toronto: Kids Can Press, 2016.

Gardy, Jennifer and Josh Holinaty. *It's Catching: The Infectious World of Germs and Microbes.* Toronto: Owlkids, 2014.

Kay, Edward and Mike Shiell. *Stinky Science: Why the Smelliest Smells Smell So Smelly.* Toronto: Kids Can Press, 2019.

Mould, Steve. *The Bacteria Book: The Big World of Really Tiny Microbes.* New York: DK Publishing, 2018.

For my children, Alex and Mika, who helped me build my immune system into the powerhouse that it is today — E.K.

To my dad, Jack. Whenever I see a perfectly planted field, a sturdy steer or a classic old tractor, I'll think of you. — M.S.

Text © 2021 Edward Kay
Illustrations © 2021 Mike Shiell

Published in Canada and the U.S. by Kids Can Press Ltd.
25 Dockside Drive, Toronto, ON M5A 0B5

Kids Can Press is a Corus Entertainment Inc. company

www.kidscanpress.com

The artwork in this book was drawn by pencil and completed in Photoshop. The text is set in Bulmer.

Edited by Kathleen Keenan
Designed by Marie Bartholomew

Printed and bound in Shenzhen, China, in 3/2021 by C & C Offset

CM 21 0 9 8 7 6 5 4 3 2 1

FSC
www.fsc.org
MIX
Paper from responsible sources
FSC® C008047

Library and Archives Canada Cataloguing in Publication

Title: Germy science : the sick truth about getting sick (and staying healthy) / written by Edward Kay ; illustrated by Mike Shiell.

Names: Kay, Edward, author. | Shiell, Mike, illustrator.

Description: Series statement: A gross science book

Identifiers: Canadiana 20200366580 | ISBN 9781525304125 (hardcover)

Subjects: LCSH: Bacteria — Juvenile literature. | LCSH: Microorganisms — Juvenile literature. | LCSH: Germ theory of disease — Juvenile literature. | LCSH: Diseases — Juvenile literature. | LCSH: Health — Juvenile literature.

Classification: LCC QR74.8 .K39 2021 | DDC j579.3 — dc23

Kids Can Press gratefully acknowledges that the land on which our office is located is the traditional territory of many nations, including the Mississaugas of the Credit, the Anishnabeg, the Chippewa, the Haudenosaunee and the Wendat peoples, and is now home to many diverse First Nations, Inuit and Métis peoples.

We thank the Government of Ontario, through Ontario Creates; the Ontario Arts Council; the Canada Council for the Arts; and the Government of Canada for supporting our publishing activity.